To:

*For Pop, who taught
me the comfort of words*

Copyright © 1994
Peter Pauper Press, Inc.
202 Mamaroneck Avenue
White Plains, NY 10601
All rights reserved
ISBN 0-88088-589-0
Printed in Hong Kong
7 6 5 4 3 2 1

WORDS

of

COMFORT

The world can be a harsh place,

which is why

you must soften its edges.

Softening the edges is what this collection of gentle thoughts is all about. It's designed to help you deal with everyday challenges by taking a fresh look at your life and asking yourself new and empowering questions. *The answers will come*, it reminds you, *if you're there to greet them.*

In matters of love, family, friendship, and work, the collection encourages you to take control of your life and thoughts, to turn life's stumbling blocks into stepping stones.

Life is a book and you are its author.
You determine its plot and pace, and
you—only you—turn its pages.

As you turn these pages, take the words of
comfort to heart and mind. Let them serve as
loving, accepting, tell-it-to-you-straight
kinds of friends. Seek their counsel and their
wisdom. Most of all, let them serve as your
mirror, reflecting the special person you are
and will always be.

—B. M. C.

Lilium Elegans var Incomparabile

1

*H*EALING

TAKES TIME—AND A BIT OF

FAITH AND COURAGE.

―――――― ↦ↂↈ ――――――

2

*T*HE PAST WAS.

TOMORROW MAY *BE*.

ONLY TODAY *IS*.

3

*F*AITH

IS THE CORNERSTONE

ON WHICH

ALL GREAT LIVES ARE BUILT.

———————— Șș ————————

4

*T*HERE IS

MUCH BEAUTY

IN THE WORLD, IF ONLY

WE'D LOOK

BEYOND OUR PROBLEMS.

5

𝒟ON'T BE
FRUSTRATED BY YOUR
INEXPERIENCE—ALL GREEN THINGS
INEVITABLY GROW.

6

𝒯HE ANSWERS
WILL COME, IF YOU'RE
THERE
TO GREET THEM.

7

*Y*OUR PROBLEMS

WILL PASS, BUT

YOU ARE HERE TO STAY.

8

*I*F THE FUTURE SEEMS

OVERWHELMING, REMEMBER

THAT IT COMES

ONE MOMENT AT A TIME.

9

WHEN YOU
FIND YOUR LIFE
FULL OF STUMBLING BLOCKS,
TURN THEM INTO
STEPPING STONES.

———————— ∼ ————————

10

FORGIVENESS
GIVES YOU THE MUCH-NEEDED
PERMISSION, ENERGY, AND FREEDOM
TO MOVE ON.

Aster Amellus

11

*I*F YOU DON'T
KNOW THE ANSWER,
PERHAPS YOU SHOULD
REPHRASE THE
QUESTION.

∞

12

*N*O ONE
CAN REJECT YOU
IF YOU ACCEPT
YOURSELF.

13

WHEN YOUR MIND

IS FULL OF INDECISION,

TRY THINKING

WITH YOUR HEART.

———— ∽∾ ————

14

ANXIETY IS

LIKE A TRAFFIC JAM;

SOMETIMES YOU HAVE TO

SIT IT OUT.

15

THE WORLD CAN BE
A HARSH PLACE,
WHICH IS WHY YOU MUST
SOFTEN ITS EDGES.

16

BE LIKE THE BIRDS;
SING AFTER EVERY STORM.

17

*I*F YOU MUST PLEASE EVERYONE,

AT LEAST PLEASE YOURSELF

ONCE IN A WHILE.

18

*L*ET YOUR DREAMS

BE YOUR NORTH STAR.

19

DON'T LET
YOUR FEAR OF
REJECTION MAKE YOU
REJECT YOUR
POSSIBILITIES.

———— ᴄᴏᴏᴄ ————

20

LIFE IS
CHANCE,
NOTHING ELSE.

Lilium Cordifolium

21

*S*HOULD YOU
MEET RESISTANCE,
TAKE COMFORT—IT'S
A GREAT WAY TO
BUILD MUSCLE.

———————— ❧ ————————

22

*T*HE GREATEST
REVENGE IS
TO ACCOMPLISH
WHAT OTHERS SAY
YOU CANNOT DO.

23

*O*PPORTUNITY
OFTEN COMES DISGUISED
IN WORK CLOTHES.

24

*I*F YOU DON'T
TAKE CONTROL
OF YOUR LIFE,
DON'T COMPLAIN
WHEN OTHERS DO.

25

*H*OPE AND ACTION ARE

TWO DISTINCT CREATURES.

ONE PURRS, THE OTHER ROARS.

26

*W*HEN THE

GOING GETS TOUGH,

SOFTEN IT WITH A HEARTFELT TALK

WITH A FRIEND.

27

*L*ET THE JUDGE

IN YOUR HEART

DETERMINE WHAT IS

RIGHT OR WRONG.

28

*D*ON'T REGRET

WHAT MIGHT HAVE BEEN.

ACCEPT WHAT IS AND REJOICE

IN WHAT IS YET TO BE.

29

*L*IFE IS A BOOK

AND YOU ARE ITS AUTHOR.

YOU DETERMINE ITS PLOT AND PACE,

AND YOU—ONLY YOU—TURN

ITS PAGES.

30

*D*ON'T HOLD

ONTO OLD DREAMS

SO TIGHT THAT YOU

CAN'T REACH FOR

NEW ONES.

Rosa Rubiginosa

31

𝒮UCCESS

COMES ONLY WITH

A LONG

TRACK RECORD.

32

𝒥N LIFE,

AS IN BASEBALL,

GETTING ON BASE

CAN BE JUST AS IMPORTANT

AS HITTING A

HOME RUN.

33

To ACCEPT YOUR FEARS
AND TO MOVE IN SPITE
OF THEM—SHAKY KNEES AND
ALL—THAT'S TRUE COURAGE.

34

We HAVE TWO BIRTHDAYS:
ONE MARKS OUR ENTRY
INTO THE WORLD, THE OTHER OUR
REENTRY INTO A WORLD
OF OUR OWN MAKING.

35

If YOU CAN'T
BE YOURSELF,
WHO DO YOU THINK
YOU CAN BE?

36

Don't FORGET
THE THREE R'S:
REST, REPLENISHMENT, AND
REFLECTION.

37

*D*ON'T WAIT

FOR THE WORLD TO CHANGE.

CHANGE IT YOURSELF.

38

*C*ONFIDENCE

IS NOT A GIFT

BUT A RIGHT

THAT MUST BE EARNED.

39

*F*EAR—ANOTHER
FOUR-LETTER WORD
THAT SHOULD BE
STRICKEN FROM
OUR VOCABULARIES.

40

*F*OLLOW
YOUR HEART
THE WAY SAILORS
FOLLOW THE
STARS.

Lilium Croceum

41

*K*NOWLEDGE

IS A SALVE

THAT SOOTHES

MANY A FEAR.

42

*I*F YOU

WANT TO EMBRACE

ALL THAT IS

GOOD IN THE WORLD,

HUG YOUR CHILD.

43

*Y*ESTERDAY
DOES NOT HAVE A
LOCK ON TODAY.
WHAT YOU DO TODAY
IS THE KEY.

——— ❧ ———

44

*I*N A WORLD OF
OVER-ACHIEVERS,
REMEMBER THAT
IT'S O.K. TO BE
JUST AVERAGE.

45

*I*F AT FIRST
YOU DON'T SUCCEED—TRY
SETTING MORE REALISTIC
EXPECTATIONS.

46

*D*O GREAT THINGS
IN YOUR LIFE,
BUT DO SMALL THINGS
AS WELL.

47

$\mathcal{T}$IME IS NOT

A COMPETITOR TO RACE AGAINST

BUT A FRIEND WITH WHOM YOU CAN

TAKE A LEISURELY WALK.

48

$\mathcal{W}$HEN LOVED ONES PASS AWAY,

BRING THEM BACK

THROUGH LOVING MEMORIES.

49

WE WILL DIE ONE DAY;

OVER THIS WE HAVE NO CHOICE.

BUT WILL WE LIVE TODAY?

THAT CHOICE IS OURS.

ఆ◎ఏ

50

LOVE DEMANDS

THAT WE BECOME

COURAGEOUS EXPLORERS.

HOW ELSE COULD WE COPE

WITH SO MUCH

UNCHARTED TERRITORY?

Lilium Auratum

51

*L*OVE
MAKES THE WORLD
GO ROUND—BUT
NOT WITHOUT FITS
AND STARTS.

———— ◈ ————

52

*T*HERE'S NOTHING
WRONG WITH BEING
REALISTIC—AS LONG AS
YOU CREATE YOUR
OWN REALITY.

53

*D*ON'T STRIVE

TO BE BETTER THAN OTHERS;

STRIVE TO BE BETTER THAN

YOUR BEST SELF.

———————— ∞ ————————

54

*J*UST BECAUSE

OTHERS DON'T EMBRACE YOUR IDEAS

DOESN'T MEAN THAT YOU TOO

SHOULD TURN A COLD SHOULDER

TO THEM.

55

*B*EING BUSY

DOESN'T NECESSARILY MEAN

YOU ARE BEING

PRODUCTIVE.

56

*D*ON'T FALL

INTO LOVE. STEP INTO IT ON

TWO STEADY FEET.

57

*O*NLY

PERFECT PEOPLE FIND

THE PERFECT MATE.

58

*Y*OU CAN'T GO HOME AGAIN,

BUT THERE'S NOTHING WRONG

WITH VISITING

WHEN YOU NEED SOME TLC.

59

$\mathcal{B}$EING ALONE

IS SCARY,

BUT NOT AS SCARY AS

FEELING ALONE IN

A RELATIONSHIP.

———————— ∽∞∽ ————————

60

$\mathcal{S}$OMETIMES

YOU HAVE TO

GO TO EXTREMES

TO ESTABLISH A

MIDDLE GROUND.

Lencojum Aestivum

61

*L*EARNING TO LOVE AGAIN

IS LIKE LEARNING TO WALK.

YOU FEAR FALLING ON YOUR FACE

YET YOU ARE GIDDY WITH

THE JOY OF COVERING

NEW GROUND.

62

*W*HEN

OLD HABITS

ARE HARD TO BREAK,

TRY BENDING THEM.

63

*S*OMETIMES

YOU MUST END AN OLD RELATIONSHIP

TO BEGIN A NEW

ONE—WITH YOURSELF.

∽∾

64

*M*ONEY

DOES NOT HAVE TO BE AN EVIL.

IT CAN ALSO BE THE

PAPER ON WHICH YOU SKETCH YOUR

LIFE'S DREAMS.

65

*T*HERE ARE

NO IMPOSSIBLE DREAMS, JUST

OUR LIMITED PERCEPTION OF

WHAT IS POSSIBLE.

66

*L*ISTENING

REQUIRES THE USE OF OUR HEARTS

AS WELL AS OUR EARS.

67

*P*ATIENCE IS
A SKILL, PERSEVERANCE
AN ART.

68

A SENSE OF HUMOR,
LIKE A TRUE FRIEND,
SEES YOU THROUGH
BAD TIMES.

69

*S*OMETIMES
THE MOST FORCEFUL STATEMENT
YOU CAN MAKE IS TO
REMAIN SILENT.

------ ∽∽∽ ------

70

*D*ON'T AVOID
A GOOD ARGUMENT, JUST
A BAD ONE.

Lilium Bulbiferum

71

*S*MALL STEPS AND
GREAT STRIDES BOTH
PROPEL YOU FORWARD.

72

*T*O MAKE UP
FOR LOST TIME, COMMIT TO
LIVING IN THE PRESENT.

73

*A*POLOGIZE, DON'T AGONIZE.

74

*I*T IS IN THE

COMPANY OF A GOOD FRIEND

THAT THE HEART

FINDS A HOME.

—— ❧ ——

75

*T*HE ONLY

TRUE FAILURE

IS THE PERSON WHO

FAILS TO TRY.

76

THERE IS NO NEED

TO FIGHT FOR YOUR PRINCIPLES.

LIVE UP TO THEM INSTEAD.

77

WE CANNOT PREDICT

THE INEVITABLE. WE CAN

ONLY ACCEPT IT.

78

*H*URTS WILL LAST FOREVER

IF YOU KEEP PICKING AT

YOUR WOUNDS.

79

*P*OTENTIAL IS NOT

SOMETHING YOU HAVE TO LIVE UP TO,

BUT IT IS SOMETHING

YOU MUST USE.

80

*L*IFE IS
AN OBSTACLE COURSE,
AND TOO OFTEN WE ARE ITS
MAJOR OBSTACLES.

————————— ∽∾ —————————

81

*G*OOD HEALTH
IS NOTHING TO
SNEEZE AT.

Lilium Monadelphum

82

*S*OMETIMES

THE HARDEST THING TO DO

IS TO DO

NOTHING AT ALL.

83

*B*ELIEVE

LIFE IS GOOD

AND YOUR LIFE WILL

NEVER BE BAD.

84

*I*F YOU WANT
LADY LUCK IN YOUR LIFE,
OPEN A DOOR FOR
HER TO ENTER.

———— ∽∽ ————

85

*C*HANGE
IS SCARY, ESPECIALLY
TO THOSE WHO WATCH US
CHANGE WHILE THEIR LIVES
STAY THE SAME.

86

*W*ORK OUT

TO WORK THROUGH

A PROBLEM.

87

*I*T'S NOT ENOUGH

TO GET WHAT YOU WANT;

YOU MUST

WANT WHAT YOU GET.

88

*Y*OU CAN'T CHANGE

THAT WHICH

YOU CAN'T ACCEPT.

89

*D*ON'T HANG OUT

WITH NEGATIVE PEOPLE,

INCLUDING YOURSELF.

90

*T*O HAVE A
SATISFYING RELATIONSHIP WITH
YOUR FAMILY, FRIENDS, AND
COLLEAGUES, YOU MUST FIRST
HAVE A SATISFYING RELATIONSHIP
WITH YOURSELF.

91

*Y*OU DON'T NEED
A LOUD VOICE TO BE HEARD.
ALL YOU NEED IS SOMETHING
WORTHWHILE TO SAY.

Rosa Indica

92

YOU CAN LIVE A HIGH LIFE

AND STILL

KEEP A LOW PROFILE.

— ⋧⋦ —

93

YOU MAY BE

DISAPPOINTED IF YOU FAIL,

BUT YOU ARE *CERTAIN*

TO BE DISAPPOINTED

IF YOU NEVER TRY.

94

*S*ET YOUR OWN STANDARDS,

AND MAKE THOSE THE ONLY SET

YOU LIVE BY.

∽∾

95

*O*NE RELAXING DAY

OFTEN DOES MORE GOOD

THAN A WEEK OF

BUSTLING ACTIVITY.

*C*ARRYING AROUND

OLD BAGGAGE WILL MAKE EVEN THE

STRONGEST PERSON STUMBLE.

97

*K*EEP YOUR EYES

PEELED ON THE FUTURE AND

YOU'LL MISS OUT ON THE SUBTLE

PLEASURES OF TODAY.

98

*M*AKE FRIENDS
WITH YOUR FEARS,
FOR IN AN EVER-CHANGING WORLD
THEY WILL BE YOUR
CONSTANT COMPANIONS.

99

*O*NLY WITH
UNDERSTANDING CAN THERE
BE FORGIVENESS.